OSIRIS

13

universal laws

Osiris in conversations with Illia

Forlag: BoD · Books on Demand,
Postboks 354 Sentrum, 0101 Oslo,
bod@bod.no
Trykk: Libri Plureos GmbH,
Friedensallee 273, 22763 Hamburg,
Tyskland
ISBN: 978-82-938-7317-4

Proof reading:

Christine Mathiesen

New Moon May 20, 2023

Today Osiris will begin channeling to me the universal laws.

My channelings with Osiris, who is my life mission soul, are done by him using my voice and me recording our conversations on the phone.

Remember, they are using my voice and my limiting language. And our names are automatically mentioned in our conversations. And then you Can feel Osiris's energy.

Have been told not to make any changes, otherwise you will not share in all his love energy from the conversations!

Osiris says that when we channel great wisdom from the highest masters, we hear the voice in the heart! Everything we hear in our head or in our energy field comes from ancient wisdom!

Osiris says there are 13 laws that rule the universe.

Law #1, what law is it, Osiris?

Universal Law 1

Attraction

It's the law of attraction, Illia, this is a very important law. And means that you attract everything you believe in, and everything you focus on you attract. This law attracts more of everything you believe in, everything you think, say and everything you feel.

What you want to experience that you are ready for will come.
Wishes will come when you are ready to receive them, if you believe in it.

Is it on another levels too, Osiris?

On many levels, Illia

What do you mean?

I believe that you develop based on how you believe you can develop.

I know faith can move mountains, but is this in a different way?
Is there anything more about Law No. 1 that you would like to share?

No, now comes law no. 2.

Universal Law 2

Cause and effect

Isn't it the same as nr. 1, Osiris?

No, it's not quite the same, Illia.
Cause and effect is that you attract more experiences based on your experiences!

If I believe that I am not good enough, then I will experience it further.

It's not exactly how it is.

What do you mean, Osiris?

I meen på norsk(mener) that the reason that comes after the experience is on a completely different level. On a physical level.

Do you mean the physical body?

I do, Illia.

So cause and effect come in the body.

I will explain it in a slightly different way.

I want to tell you about an experience you've had, Illia, and what you've created from it. After the big traumatic experience, you were completely devastated.

Yes, I felt I lost the right to determine (bestemmelsesrett) my own body.

And what it creates is tension in the muscles and joints, physical and psychological problems.

Yes, I know all about that.

You do, but what you don't know, Illia, is that it's on another level as well.

What level, Osiris?

You spread that experience out on earth.

What?

Yes, your faith after the experience spreads beyond the whole earth and the whole universe, Illia.

So my faith spreads to everyone else around me?

Absolutely.

So it's not just the family that goes to?

No, it gods to everyone.

Oh, so fierce, Osiris, now I'm sad.

Yes, it is very important to know this.
Working with thoughts after experiences and getting them out of the way right away is very, very important.

Oh, God, I didn't know that.

Faith after the experiences we experience spreads to all people on earth?

It does, dear.

Universal Law No. 3

Forgiveness

The Law of Forgiveness?

Yes. If you forgive, you lift up all of humanity and the entire universe, Illia.

What is the best way to forgive?

Forgive yourself for attracting all that has been attracted.
And forgive people for being themselves.

Is there more to law nr. 3?

Yes, Illia, there's a lot more to it, you understand.
It is the law that whatever you forgive is released from the universe.

Does it really, Osiris?

It certainly does, but it's important to forgive in the right way.

What do you mean by that, Osiris?

To forgive in the right way is to free all people on earth, Illia, from sin, guilt and shame.

Wow!

Yes, there is a lot there, Illia. The religions destroy a lot.

I know that. The priest made me feel like a sinner already at the age of six!

I know you know, Illia, this law here is important. It is important that you forgive yourself, and have thought what you have thought, when you have thought it. Move on and forgive it and it will disappear from the universe. This way you don't have to create it with others. So take it at once, after an experience.

Universal Law No. 4

Acceptance

What is meant by that law, Osiris?

**This law, Illia, is about giving acceptance to get acceptance!
When we accept others as they are, we too will encounter acceptance in our lives.
So when we judge others, we ourselves are judged by our own yardstick!**

So what is the easiest way to accept someone else's way of being?
Does this also apply to acts of acceptance?

**It certainly does, Illia.
The easiest way to accept others is to say to yourself: "It's their way of living. Mine is completely different, and everyone has the right to go their own way."**

How can we manage to let go of condemnation?
We get it in with mother's milk - look at them, he's so strange, etc.

Act with the thoughts and feelings you don't want to bring in from your story/aura.
Say, "bye!" and wave it away!

Acceptance is a release from judgment on earth regarding all human races and reality.

It is only when we manage to accept everyone as equal that there will be peace and paradise on earth.

Universal Law No. 5

Attraction

The law of attraction is on many levels.
The most important plane is consideration.

What do you mean by consideration as attraction, Osiris?

Mindfulness (omtanke)with attraction, Illia, is a very important resource that most people don't know about.
That law means that everything you attract you have created yourself. You know that, Illia.

Yes. Consideration. What do you think, Osiris?
I do not understand what you mean.

Consideration is part of attraction.
When you are considerate of things, people and living beings around you, you attract back that they are considerate of you.

Is that the whole law of attraction?

That's it, dear.

Does it have to do with what you believe you attract?

No, it is the law of creation.

Are you done with Law No. 5, do you want to elaborate?

No, there's no need, Illia.

Universal Law No. 6

Forgiveness on a higher level

It is possible to forgive on many levels

What do you mean, Osiris?

You can forgive on a much higher level than just humanity, Illia.

I don't understand what you mean, Osiris.

No, I can understand that, it's not that easy to understand.
Will try to explain it, Illia.
When you forgive on a higher level, you free the entire universe, Illia.

The entire universe, including the dark planets?

Absolutely.

So if we forgive all the aliens and all that, then we free all the universes?

You do, Illia.

Okay, so how do we forgive on a higher plane then, Osiris?

To forgive on a higher level, you must be in the moment (nuet) when you forgive.
Be in the moment and address all the universes at once, Illia.

What do you want me to say, Osiris?

I want you to be in the present when you say:

HERE AND NOW I INVOCATE ALL DEMONS FROM ALL DIMENSIONS AND REALITIES.

Then you say, "How does it feel for you to be forgiven and to be one with the soul in your hearts? Amen."

This is how the universes are cleansed of darkness and evil.

We can't handle all the universes at once, can we?

Yes, some of them, Illia.

Wow, thanks Osiris!
It was a very strong experience, thank you.

Universal Law No. 7

Trust

To attract the good in life, it is important to have trust.
Because trust creates the good in life, Illia.

Is it Universal Law No. 7?

Absolutely.
You have built up a trust in Seraphim and me over many years, and it is solid.
The only thing you don't really trust is Seraphim with enough nourishment, and that's coming now, you see.
So relax completely and have confidence in it now.
Have confidence in it now.

What else do you want to tell about trust, Osiris?

That is, when you build up 100% confidence that you deserve ONLY the best in life, Illia,
then it will come to you, you understand.

How will I manage to build up such trust, Osiris?

You should just know that it is me and Seraphim who give it to you, Illia..

Then I have full confidence, Osiris.

Do you actually have it?

I feel that way. I have full confidence in you, Osiris. The only thing you have no idea about are dates and years. And Seraphim has struggled to give me enough nourishment, but it is the first time he is one with his physical body. He has failed a few times, but now he seems to be able to keep a balance of what I need.
On all other levels, I have full confidence in you. I really have full confidence in you, dear.

Then you can start to attract many people, Illia, on a high level.

How do we do it, Osiris? Surely there is a special technique with that law?

**It certainly is, Illia.
You have to want to experience it, dare to experience it and know that it is yours.**

Ok, how am I supposed to work it up?

**You have to start by creating something you really want and need, Illia.
So then it's easier; when you get what you really want and really need, and what you really need to experience.
When you experience that, Illia, the rest will come much easier afterwards, you see.
So don't wish, think of something you want to experience that you don't yet know what it is. Think of something you know what it is and create it first, then you know it works. Then you build up even stronger trust, dear, because then you know it works.**

It is strong, Osiris.

But then it's completely automatic, Illia.

Oh, thanks, honey, that sounds magical.
Is there anything more you want to say about Act No. 7?

Yes, it is a magic law, a magic law and it works on all levels at once.

What do you mean?

It works on that level, Illia, which is on the second level away from the physical, you understand.
You can create in the physical, but you have to work in the non-physical.

Thank you, Osiris.

Universal Law No. 8

Satisfaction

To satisfy the right desires.

So exciting, Osiris. Which are the right desires to satisfy?

**There is wisdom and recognition of wisdom.
Desire for satisfaction on the spiritual level.
Desire for satisfaction on a human level without satisfying the ego.**

Is there anything more, Osiris?

**It is very important to satisfy the desires of the soul.
Work every day on the satisfaction of the desires of the soul.**

Is this what the law is about?

That's it, dear.

Would you like to tell more about Law No. 8, Osiris.

I want to tell you that this is an important law, even if it looks very mundane. Then it goes deep and affects all the universes at once.

Everything does, right?

It does. With everything we think, say and do, we create fluctuations that go out to everything. It is very important to know what you are doing, to be aware.

That I understand. What will you tell next, Osiris?
So when one satisfies oneself on the right desires, the good, creative energy spreads to all the universes?

It certainly does, Illia. It is very important to know, you see, to know that you are satisfying the right desires.
Otherwise you abuse your own life force, by satisfying the physical ego desires.

Then you only satisfy the ego and not your own vitality, and are drained every time.

Oh, that was hard to hear, Osiris.

I know, but the people need to hear it, dear. Because they want to satisfy so many desires that it goes beyond everything. (Går utover altet alt sammen)

I understand, Osiris. Is there more you want to tell?

No. The important thing to know is that things spread.
You are not alone in the universes, you are one with everything, so know it now!

Thank you, Osiris.

Universal Law No. 9

Satisfaction on the spiritual level

Oh, so exciting, tell!

**The law is that you should seek out what you want to experience, in the spiritual.
You have to want to experience it, to be able to see it.
And you have to believe in it, Illia, as the saying goes, faith moves mountains and so much, much more.
So the belief in what you want to experience creates what you want to experience.**

So strong. Is there anything else you would like to say about the law?

No, that is the most important thing about this law, Illia, and it is very important that those who want a spiritual life must want to know, and know that they deserve it and really believe that it exists in order to

experience the spiritual life in their full moons. (Fulle monn)

Thank you, Osiris!

Universal Law No. 10

Worship

Worship, what is meant by that law, Osiris?

To worship something outside oneself is sacrilege!(helligbrøde)

When you have GOD inside you, in your own closet.(lønnkammer)
A light that is so big, much bigger than any other light you can bring in from outside.

So the worship must become worshiping your own, inner core. The only true worship, amen!

Is there anything else you want to say about the law?

It is a very important law.
As soon as you worship something outside your own body, the life force passes to what/whom you worship.

It was hard to hear, so all the people Who worship Jesus and Gurus loose their life force!

But so it is, dear sister.
When we worship things, we distance ourselves from our own body.
And we are open to everything that will take up residence and everything that will shake(rokke) the energy in the body, while we send our life force over to what we worship.
Therefore, it is important to only worship one's own, inner core, our own, inner Christ-light.

Was it all about Law no 10, Osiris?

That was it, a simple and beautiful law.

Universal Law No. 11

Positioning

What would you like to share about Law No. 11, Osiris?

It's a magical law, Illia, like any other law.
It is the law of positioning.

Now I don't understand what you mean.

To position oneself where it is right to be at all times. Perform the right actions at all times, place yourself where you belong.

I still don't quite understand what you mean, Osiris.

It is not so easy to understand illia, but is just as important as the other laws, you see.
If you go out to places you are not supposed to be, then there will be an imbalance in the energies in the universe illia.

Wow?

Yes, thats how it is, dear.
Following intuition is the alpha and omega of keeping the balance in the universes.
When you go against your intuition, you create an imbalance in the energies in all the universes, Illia.

Really, Osiris, is what we're doing so serious?

These are very serious things you are dealing with.
What you do is much more important than what you may think it is.
Remember, you have all heard that all is one, all are connected in the oneness, the all.
God is all in all, everything.
Ergo, everything we do or don't do, or where we are or aren't, affects the whole in balance in all the universes.

I understand what you're saying, but I don't quite understand that it can be so incredibly important what we choose.

Choosing the right thing is the alpha and omega of a person's life. Remember we are all angels.
When we choose away from the angel, we destroy the balance in all the universes.

So sad, sounds bad.

I know it sounds bad, Illia, but it's important that you know. So you can learn to follow the right path.

That I understand. Is there more you want to tell about the law, Osiris?

No, it was all about that law. No need to supplement it any more.

But would you like to explain more so that it will be easier for us to understand the law?

Say you get an inner feeling about going to Africa, then you choose to go somewhere else instead.

What happens then?

You create an imbalance by not going to Africa.

But what happens if I choose to go somewhere else instead of Africa, what happens in my life?

A lot happens in your life, you're going the wrong way, Illia.
That's why you also get the wrong experiences on that journey that you wouldn't have had if you had traveled with your intuition, dear.

Is that what you mean!

So it affects not only you, but everything in the universe, creates an imbalance in everything, in the energies.

That's so hard to hear, Osiris.

Yes. There we have the unit and everything, you know, dear.

Universal Law No. 12

Attraction on the spiritual plane

Is it different from the regular law of attraction?

Very different, Illia.
Here you can attract help from other realities, planets and dimensions.

That sounds good, Osiris. What can you tell us more about the law?

This is a very powerful law. By powerful I mean a law of fulfillment in the spiritual attraction.

How do we do that?

One frees oneself from the physical reality, in order to attract the spiritual experiences.

Then one needs to be in the present, away from the physical body, inside the heart chakra, perfectly present.

What else should one do, after one has entered the present within the chakra?

Ask for what you need to experience. And then one must really want to experience on the spiritual plane. In all possible ways, in all possible variations and the spiritual life, you can then attract yourself when you are in the present, one with your soul inside your heart.
Because when you are in the present in the heart chakra, you are one with your soul. Ergo, the attraction on the spiritual plane becomes much stronger than just ordinary attraction on the physical plane.

Is there anything more you want to say about Act No. 12?

Much more, Illia. We need to take this law here very carefully, you see, because this law here is very important.

You do it as you worship yourself, inside your heart chamber, in your own Christ energy.
And then attracts the spiritual experiences one needs to experience in order to progress on the path within one's heart chakra, one with one's soul.

Thank you, Osiris.

Universal Law No. 13

Creation

What do you mean by that, Osiris?

You yourself create every day with your thoughts that become reality.
It is a law that executes and creates everything you think about each day, to become reality the next day, the next day, and the next day.
Not just here on earth, but in all realities and dimensions.

Oh, God, is it such a strong law, dear?

You know that you are all one, and all connected, and what you believe in you create for yourself and everything else.
You must be very careful what you believe, dear ones.

Awesome to know.

Is there more to tell of the law, Osiris?

No, it's not, dear, but it's a very important law, you understand.

It's a magical law, so when you think loving thoughts and believe in love on earth, you spread love to everything and all the universes at once.
It is you who have to lift yourself up, no one else can do it.

You think you can get help from other planets, but that's nonsense, it doesn't work.

It is you who will lift the earth, it is you who are the angels who are down here to lift the dimension of the earth.
AMEN!

Is there more you want to tell, Osiris?

No, it's very important.
Law No. 13 is the most important of all the laws.

Thank you dear Osiris for your wisdom of the Universal Laws.

Would love to share my other channeled books.

"Bullied into love"

"Osiris Book 1"
"1 with the soul"
"Planets and Realities"
"Angels of the Elements"
"Osiris 13. universal laws"

Feel free to ask questions by email
«aandevokter@gmail.com

Good luck living the magical and important 13 Laws!